Table of Contents

by Phyllis Pellman Good and Rachel Thomas Pellman.

International Standard Book Number: 1-56148-154-8.
Printed in the United States of America. Design by Dawn J. Ranck.

Baked Chicken and Rice

Makes 6-8 servings

$^{1}/_{2}$ cup plus 1 Tbsp. butter or margarine, melted
$^{1}/_{2}$ cup mushrooms, chopped
$^{1}/_{4}$ cup celery, chopped
$^{1}/_{2}$ cup plus 1 Tbsp. flour
1 Tbsp. salt
$^{1}/_{4}$ tsp. pepper
$4^{1}/_{2}$ cups milk
$1^{1}/_{3}$ cups water
1 cup long grain rice, uncooked
Dash of garlic salt
6-8 seasoned chicken parts

1. Add mushrooms and celery to melted butter in saucepan and sauté until golden. Stir in flour and seasonings. Gradually add milk and bring to the boiling point, stirring constantly until thickened. Remove from heat.
2. Blend in water. Add rice and garlic salt, mixing well.
3. Pour into large roaster or baking pan. Arrange chicken pieces on top of rice mixture.
4. Cover and bake 3 hours at 300°.

Chicken Corn Pie

Makes 6-8 servings

1 stewing chicken
1 qt. corn, cooked
Pastry enough for 2 double-crust pies

1. Cook chicken and remove from bones. Make a thin gravy with the chicken stock.
2. Line 2 9" pie plates with pastry. Place meat and corn in alternate layers in crust. Add gravy enough to barely cover chicken-corn mixture. Cover with crust and seal edges. Bake at 425° for 20 minutes. Eat hot with remaining gravy.

Variations:

1. Delete 3 cups corn. In place of corn add cooked carrots, peas, and cubed potatoes.
2. Beef Vegetable Pie—follow above procedure but substitute $1\frac{1}{2}$ lb. beef in place of chicken. Cook beef until tender. Cube and follow procedure using beef broth. Use 1 cup each peas, carrots, potatoes, and corn, cooked.

Chicken Spaghetti

Makes 12 servings

1 stewing chicken
3 Tbsp. butter or margarine
6 celery stems, chopped
2 onions, chopped
1/4 cup mushrooms, chopped
3 Tbsp. flour
1 cup milk
1/2 lb. sharp cheese, grated
1 pint chicken stock
1 Tbsp. Worcestershire sauce
Salt and pepper to taste
1/2 lb. spaghetti
1 small bottle stuffed olives, chopped or sliced
1 cup pecans, chopped

1. Cook chicken in water until tender. Remove from bones and cut in large pieces. Reserve stock.
2. Melt butter. Sauté celery, onions, and mushrooms until tender. Add flour and stir to form a smooth paste. Gradually add milk. Stir until thickened. Add cheese. Stir until melted. Add chicken stock and seasonings.
3. Cook spaghetti in water for 3 minutes. Drain. Add to

stock mixture and let stand for 1 hour. Mix in chicken and olives.

4. Pour into a 9" x 15" shallow casserole. Top with pecans. Bake at 350° for 1/2 hour.

Variation:

Add 2 cups cooked peas and carrots

Country Chicken Supper

Makes 8 servings

4 ozs. spaghetti, uncooked
1 lb. mild cream cheese, cubed or grated
1 cup milk
1/2 cup mayonnaise
2 cups cooked chicken (or turkey) cubed
1 1/2 cups peas and carrots, cooked

1. Cook spaghetti. Drain and set aside.
2. Heat cheese, milk, and mayonnaise together over low heat, stirring until sauce is smooth.
3. Add chicken, vegetables, and spaghetti to sauce, mixing well. Pour into 2-quart casserole.
4. Bake at 350° for 35-40 minutes.

Lazy Day Stew

Makes 8 servings

2 lbs. beef cubes
2 cups carrots, sliced
2 cups potatoes, diced
2 medium onions, sliced
1 cup celery, chopped
1½ cups green beans
2 tsp. quick cooking tapioca
1 Tbsp. salt
½ tsp. pepper
8 oz. can tomato sauce
1 cup water
1 Tbsp. brown sugar

1. Place raw beef cubes (do not brown) in a single layer in a 2½ quart casserole or roast pan.
2. Add vegetables and/or any others you desire.
3. Sprinkle tapioca, salt, and pepper over top. Pour tomato sauce mixed with water over vegetables and seasonings.
4. Crumble brown sugar over all.
5. Cover tightly and do not peep! Bake at 325° for 3 hours.

Variation:
Stew may be made in a slow cooker.

Sausage and Apple Casserole

Makes 8 servings

1½ lbs. link sausage
  cut in small pieces, or
  1½ lbs. bulk sausage in small balls
4 medium apples, pared and sliced
3 medium sweet potatoes, pared and sliced
½ tsp. salt
1 Tbsp. flour
2 Tbsp. sugar

1. Fry sausage, saving drippings.
2. Combine salt, flour, and sugar, Arrange sausage, apples, and potatoes in layers in a casserole. Sprinkle some flour mixture over each layer. Top with a layer of sausage.
3. Sprinkle casserole with 1 Tbsp. sausage drippings. Cover tightly. Bake at 375° for 1 hour.

Truckpatch Dinner

Bacon slices
Ground beef
Potatoes
Peas
Carrots
Salt and pepper to taste

1. Arrange a layer of bacon on bottom of roast pan or casserole. Add a layer of raw hamburger. Add a layer of sliced potatoes, seasoned with salt and pepper. Bake at 375° for 1 hour.
2. Remove from oven and add a layer of peas and carrots. Return to oven and bake 45-60 minutes longer.

Variation:
Pour 1½ cups tomatoes over all before baking.

Mother's Tomato Rice Meat Pie

Makes 12 servings

1 lb. ground beef
1/4 cup green pepper, chopped
1 small onion, chopped
1/2 cup dry bread crumbs
Salt and pepper to taste
2 cups tomato sauce
1 1/3 cups minute rice
1 cup water
1 cup cheddar cheese, grated

1. Combine beef, pepper, onion, bread crumbs, salt, pepper, and 1/2 cup tomato sauce. Mix well. Pat into bottom and sides of a greased 9" square pan.
2. Combine remaining tomato sauce, rice, water, and 1/2 cup cheese. Spoon mixture into meat shell. Cover and bake at 350° for 25 minutes. Top with remaining cheese. Bake, uncovered, 10-15 minutes longer.

Stuffed Cabbage

Makes 8-10 servings

1 head cabbage with large loose leaves
1 onion, minced
1 lb. ground beef
1 cup rice, cooked
1 egg, beaten
Salt and pepper to taste
1/4 cup tomato paste
1/2 cup water
1 cup cultured sour cream

1. Remove large outer leaves (8-10) from cabbage and cook in boiling salt water for 3 minutes. Drain.
2. Brown hamburger and onion together. Stir in cooked rice, egg, salt, and pepper.
3. Place hamburger-rice mixture on cabbage leaves. Roll up and fasten with toothpicks. Place in greased baking dish.
4. Stir together tomato paste, water, and sour cream. Then pour over cabbage rolls.
5. Cover and bake at 350° for 1 hour.

Beef, Corn, and Noodles

Makes 8 servings

1 lb. hamburger, browned
1 pt. corn, cooked
2 cups noodles, cooked
2 cups beef broth
1 Tbsp. butter
3 hard-boiled eggs, diced

1. Mix together the hamburger, corn, noodles, and broth. Pour into greased baking dish.
2. Dot with butter. Sprinkle eggs over top.
3. Bake at 350° for 40-45 minutes.

Cheese Soufflé

Makes 2 servings

2 Tbsp. butter
3 Tbsp. flour
1/2 cup milk
1/2 cup cheese, grated
2 large or 3 small eggs, separated
1/2 tsp. salt

1. Melt butter. Add flour and stir to make a smooth paste. Gradually add milk. Stir until thickened. Add cheese. Stir until melted. Add egg yolks and salt.
2. Beat egg whites until stiff. Gently fold into sauce. Turn into greased casserole or soufflé dish. Bake at 325° for 25 minutes.

Baked Carrots and Apples

Makes 7 servings

4 cups carrots, cut in 1/2" pieces
3 cups apples, peeled, cored, and sliced
1/4 cup honey
2 Tbsp. butter or margarine
Paprika

1. Steam carrots until tender. Drain. Stir in apples and honey.
2. Turn into buttered casserole. Dot with butter. Cover and bake at 350° for 50 minutes.
3. Stir. Sprinkle with paprika. Bake, uncovered, an additional 10 minutes.

Scalloped Potatoes

Makes 12 servings

6 medium potatoes cooked in jackets
1/2 cup butter
1 tsp. parsley flakes
1/4 cup onion, chopped
1 tsp. dry or prepared mustard
1/4 tsp. pepper
1 tsp. salt
1/4 cup milk
1/4 cup cheese, grated

1. Dice potatoes and place in greased casserole.
2. Melt butter. Add other ingredients and cook until cheese is melted. Pour sauce over potatoes and bake at 350° for 45 minutes.

Variation: Omit cheese. Add 1 cup sour cream plus 1 lb. cooked, diced ham.

Tuna Noodle Casserole

Makes 12 servings

1 8-oz. pkg. noodles
8 Tbsp. butter
5 Tbsp. flour
$2\frac{1}{2}$ cups milk
8 oz. pkg. cream cheese
1 large can tuna
Salt and pepper to taste
6 oz. mild cheese, sliced
$1\frac{1}{2}$ cups soft bread crumbs

1. Cook noodles in water until tender. Drain and set aside.
2. Melt 5 Tbsp. of the butter. Add flour and stir to form a smooth paste. Gradually add milk and stir until thickened. Add cream cheese and tuna. Stir until cheese is melted. Add seasonings.
3. In greased casserole, layer noodles, sauce, and sliced cheese alternately.
4. Melt remaining butter. Stir in bread crumbs. Sprinkle buttered crumbs over top of casserole. Bake at 350° for 30 minutes.

Variations:

1. Use salmon in place of tuna.
2. Add 1 cup peas and 2 chopped hard-boiled eggs.

Macaroni and Cheese

Makes 6-8 servings

1½ cups milk, scalded
2 cups soft bread crumbs or cubes (whole wheat or white)
¼ cup butter or margarine, melted
1 Tbsp. onion, chopped
1½ cups mild cheese, grated or cubed
½ tsp. salt
3 eggs, separated
1½ cups macaroni, cooked
Paprika

1. Pour scalded milk over bread crumbs. Stir in butter, onion, cheese, and salt. Mix well.
2. Beat egg yolks and add. Stir in cooked macaroni.
3. Beat egg whites to form soft peaks. Fold into macaroni mixture.
4. Pour into a buttered casserole and sprinkle with paprika. Bake at 350° for 1 hour.

Macaroni Dried Beef Casserole

Makes 8 servings

3 Tbsp. butter
2 Tbsp. onion, minced
1/4 cup mushrooms, chopped
3 Tbsp. flour
2 1/2 cups milk
1 cup uncooked macaroni
1 cup cheese, cubed
2 hard-boiled eggs, chopped
1/4 lb. dried beef, chipped

1. Melt butter. Sauté onion and mushrooms until tender. Add flour and stir until smooth. Gradually add 1 cup of milk and stir until thickened. Remove from heat and stir in remaining milk.
2. Combine all other ingredients. Pour milk mixture over all. Mix well. Turn into greased casserole. Let stand 3-4 hours or overnight. Bake at 350° for 1 hour.